For everyone who's ever read the Bible
and thought, "wait, what?!"

Once upon a time, God got really mad. Not like, "I skipped breakfast" mad, more like "burn it all down and start over" mad.

With the measurements provided, the Ark would be 450x75x45 feet. It's said to have had three decks which is about 101,250 square feet total.

But Noah obeyed. He built the boat. He loaded the animals. He just had to invent;
- Industrial plumbing
- Long-distance animal transportation
- Large-scale waste management to support enough poop to fill the Mediterranean
- Climate control for penguins and camels
- A food storage system that wouldn't exist for another 4,000 years
- And HR policies for lions and gazelles sharing bunk beds

The End